The Richard III Reinterment Liturgies

An Account of the
Planning and Execution of the
Ceremonies and Liturgical Reburial of
the Bones of King Richard III in Leicester
Cathedral in Passion Week 2015

by

Johannes Arens, Alexandra Buckle,
Gordon Campbell and Tim Stratford

edited by

Tim Stratford
Archdeacon of Leicester

The cover motif is the 'RIII Logo' used by Leicester Cathedral for all printing and publishing purposes throughout the events recorded in this Study, and it is used here by permission of the Dean of Leicester Cathedral.

© Tim Stratford and the respective authors 2016
ISSN: 0951-2667
ISBN: 978-1-848-25832-7

Contents

1485 to 2015		4
Introduction		5
1	The Canvas by Tim Stratford	8
2	A Medieval Starting Point by Alexandra Buckle	19
3	The Language of Liturgy in Two Ages by Gordon Campbell	37
4	Symbol and Choreography of the Reinterment Liturgies for Richard III by Johannes Arens	51

1485

Richard III, the last king of England from the line of York, on 22 August 1485 faced his Lancastrian opponent, Henry Tudor, in the battle of Bosworth Field. Richard lost the battle and lost his life. His body was taken to Leicester and given reverent if hasty burial by the Franciscan Friars of Greyfriars. And there his body might have rested deeply covered in an unmarked place until the end of time, had it not been for a remarkable piece of detective work. Once it was unearthed, a further challenge emerged: how to set about arranging a reburial.

2015

The events of March 2015 fall within the following timetable.

Passion Week 2015	Category	Event
22 March Sunday (Passion Sunday)	*'Reception'* Procession and Reception	Procession from Market Bosworth stopping at stations en route with short offices. Reception of coffin at the cathedral font with ceremonies. Compline
23 March Monday 24 March Tuesday 25 March Wednesday (Annunciation of the BVM)	*'Repose'*	The coffin still at the font. Usual daily services of the cathedral. Visitors walking past the coffin.
26 March Thursday	*'Reinterment'*	Reinterment service – coffin moved to centre of nave, sermon preached beside it, then coffin taken to ambulatory, and reinterred in the grave there.
27 March Friday	*'Reveal'*	'Reveal' Service of the Word, a form of Evensong including Curve Theatre drama and many colours of roses, then the grave area opened to visitors Celebration in streets and gardens.

Introduction

In the summer of 2012 the mortal remains of King Richard III were extraordinarily unearthed under a council office car park in Leicester City Centre by a team from Leicester University. Much of what followed was just as unprecedented and extraordinary as the archaeological discovery had itself been. A Licence from the Ministry of Justice that permitted the removal of the remains from their original burial site required that they be reinterred in consecrated ground. Following a Judicial Review the responsibility for this fell on Leicester Cathedral, only a stone's throw away from the former Greyfriars church, dissolved in 1538, where the friars had first buried the king.

The reburial was a signal occasion without parallel in recent times and it captured the public imagination. Channel Four televised two of the services in their entirety and these were broadcast worldwide. The liturgical events carried public theology as a rare opportunity.

This Study is not so much an analysis of those liturgies as it is a resource alongside the texts[1] and journalism. The four authors were among those who had to struggle with understanding what was being asked of the church and how a Christian community should most appropriately respond through prayer and ritual. Johannes Arens, as Canon Precentor of the cathedral, was ultimately responsible for turning the liturgical ideas into acts of worship. The reburial of the king's remains included a series of events that extended well beyond the formal liturgies of the church. This is, of course, equally

---

[1] *Service of Compline, Service of Reinterment, Service of Reveal* (Leicester Cathedral, Leicester, 2015).

true of the myriad of baptisms, weddings and funerals that comprise the church's regular ministry, but in these there is a pattern and familiarity that allows many assumptions to be made. On this unique occasion there could be no such assumptions. What follows below is a working out from first principles of what the church should do and how it could be understood. The authors have tried to describe their own trains of thought as they contributed towards forming the liturgies that enabled public prayer and worship in the light of life, death and eternity through the journey of a fallen monarch.

The authors of this Study were only a part of a large team and are grateful to the many colleagues whose work made sense of what they did. They acknowledge the wisdom and skills that extended well beyond their own liturgical interests, especially in the person of the Dean of Leicester, Very Revd David Monteith. He brought a theological acumen and organizational ability that gave great coherence to something that could easily have become meaningless or even ridiculous. The list of others who should be acknowledged here is sadly too extensive to detail.

However, the four authors of this Study formed the working core of a small group established by the cathedral to develop the liturgy for the reburial service. This group, including people drawn from the church, the academy, the city and the Richard III Society, is referred to in the pages that follow as the 'Liturgy Group'. Each of the four has here contributed a chapter, each providing a distinctive perspective. While the authors share a great deal of one another's thinking they do not necessarily subscribe to everything written by the others, coming, as they do, from very different approaches to faith and tradition.

1 'The Canvas': Tim Stratford explores the big picture of public theology and the narrative developed to unfold and explore this over the course of a week.

2 'A Medieval Starting Point': Alexandra Buckle describes the discovery, translation and application of a fifteenth-century reburial

rite to an event that straddled the centuries between then and now.

3 'The Language of Liturgy in Two Ages': Gordon Campbell considers the translational and linguistic issues that were faced by a liturgical exercise committed to taking seriously the burial of a fifteenth-century king whilst maintaining the integrity of twenty-first century Church and society.

4 'Symbol and Choreography of the Reinterment Liturgies for Richard III': Johannes Arens looks at the symbols and actions that extend beyond the words, but beg similar issues of translation and appropriation in the twenty-first century as well as those that emerged from innovation.

The Rev Canon Dr Johannes Arens is Canon Precentor of Leicester Cathedral and a member of the College of Evangelists of the Church of England. His academic interests include liturgy and systematic theology, particularly theology of sin and redemption, having completed doctoral research on the theology of addiction.

Dr Alexandra Buckle (University of Oxford) is Lecturer in Music History at St Anne's College, and St Hilda's College, Oxford. She has published widely on historical and musical topics from the fifteenth and sixteenth centuries and has acted as a Consultant for English Heritage on a number of occasions.

Professor Gordon Campbell, FBA, is Fellow in Renaissance Studies and Public Orator at the University of Leicester, historical consultant to a Museum of the Bible being built in Washington, D.C., and chair of the Fabric Advisory Committee at Leicester Cathedral. His academic interests include the Bible, historical theology, and ecclesiastical history.

The Ven Dr Tim Stratford is Archdeacon of Leicester and was a member of the Church of England's Liturgical Commission from 2006 to 2015. He has an academic interest in the interconnectedness of liturgy and the Church's mission to urban communities characterized by deprivation, having completed doctoral research on the mid-Victorian Slum-Priest Ritualists.

1

The Canvas

Where do you start when you are given a responsibility to bury the human remains of a English king who died in battle 530 years ago? This was the challenge laid at the door of Leicester Cathedral in 2015. The canvas on which the cathedral had to paint was prominent, extensive and, at first, blank. For a pastoral liturgist the first response is to get the book out and see what the manual says, but there wasn't one. It might at first seem as if this just needed to be a funeral on a grand scale. But if it was to be so, then who were the mourners?

It was clear that there were going to be some present who had invested a great deal of work, and in some cases emotional energy, into restoring King Richard's reputation. This had even extended to the seemingly impossible dream of finding his remains and making restitution for his ignominious death materially as well as intellectually. And members of the Richard III Society owned a strong identity with the king. But no one present knew the man. At a funeral the Christian Church does not just help people lay to rest the physical remains of a person but it commends the deceased to God. Whilst a minister may say the words of Commendation, they are most especially prayed in the hearts of those who have shared life deeply with their loved one. Even in the most dislocated of funerals imaginable, such as one for an unknown soldier, there are those present who have shared with the victim in the struggles of comradeship and circumstances of death.

In this case it would have been wrong to conceive of what was being undertaken as a funeral. One of the earliest decisions taken was that there would be no one present who could credibly commend King Richard III to God, so there should be no Commendation. This we regarded as the principal characteristic that distinguished a funeral from any other rite involving the remains of a deceased person.

A second consideration was the evidence that the Franciscan friars of Greyfriars had already given the king a funeral of sorts. His body had been laid in a place of honour in the choir of the church, albeit hastily. Whilst there are accounts from after the battle of Bosworth that the king's body was buried 'without pompe or funeral' it is unlikely that Franciscan friars would have buried him in consecrated ground without prayer.[2] The post-battle accounts emphasize the absence of ceremonial dignity that might have been otherwise expected.

Not goodbye but hello!
Alongside such observations about what the church today was not doing lie some interesting questions about what it was doing. It became clear that this was no goodbye. Even after their reburial, the remains of the king would be more visibly present in the heart of Leicester than they ever had been before, at least since the time of Henry VIII. They had lain since his dissolution of the monasteries anonymously under ground that had endured multiple developments on the surface. Following the archaeological find the remains had been kept hidden in an undisclosed part of Leicester University throughout the identification process and right up to the week of reinterment. But now they were to become a focus for visitors to the city. Indeed over 10,000 people a day visited during the first week that the king's remains were in the cathedral.

There was a new story for the city of Leicester unfolding; a story that was given tangible reality by the emergence of the bones. This was less about the passing of somebody into history and more about their emergence into today. If a funeral is about goodbyes, the reinterment

---

[2] http://www.le.ac.uk/richardiii/faz/reinterment.html (accessed 13 March 2016).

of Richard III was a hello. The liturgies of the week somehow needed to recognize this without becoming shallow, triumphalist, commercially compromised or distasteful. The church was after all placing human remains in their final resting place and the way the King's remains were treated would speak of how the Christian church treats all human remains, whether of those who have already died or of those who were living and watching.

Whilst the Liturgy Group was trying to make sense of what they were doing, cathedral, diocesan and city leadership was working at giving sense to what was unfolding. This thinking inhabits the worlds of overarching narratives, vision statements and strap lines. The phrase 'With Dignity and Honour' was coined, and to the Liturgy Group this had a deep resonance with its struggle. It set the tone for what needed to be done.

Public Perception

A constraint on what could be done was the prevalence of public perceptions. As the historical liturgists turned to the manual of what had been done in ancient times, when the bones of a saint had been translated to a higher and more sacred place, so it seemed that the natural practice should be to gather King Richard's bones into an ornate ossuary. An ossuary rather than a coffin would avoid pretending that this was the burial of a body now in need of decay. But there were demands for a procession through the streets 'with dignity and honour', a tribute which had been denied this monarch at the time of his death. And the template was that of a human-sized coffin draped with a royal standard and carried on a gun carriage, but the casquet would look as nothing if it were the size of an ossuary, no longer in its largest dimension than a femur. It was felt this could not carry the sense of a person that a coffin would. There was something here about how people living in the current age deal with their dead that is most definitely not the same as the medieval saints of ancient times. Ritual could not simply be repeated no

The Canvas

matter what its antecedence, although some knights in shining armour did find their way into the street procession.

A competing challenge was a growing sense in some circles that Richard III should be treated as a saintly figure. But history would not allow the making of a new saint in so many ways. Somehow there needed to be a narrative that this was the reburial of somebody who was sinful and fallen like everybody else we know. Here was no model of how we should aspire to be if we seek godly living.

The need to use a coffin in this public ritual in order to help contemporary people connect with its reality was paralleled throughout the liturgy. For the same reasons a service in Latin or medieval English was inappropriate, and prayers that uncritically assumed pre-reformation politics or pre-scientific thought would have been unintelligible. It would have become meaningless to follow a rite that did not give proper recognition to how people (and institutions) needed to deal with one another and with God whilst these bones were being entrusted to the cathedral.

A Narrative of Receive, Repose, Reinter, Reveal

Four words all beginning with 're' soon came to describe the overarching narrative. The narrative was more important than the words, though the convenience of an initial alliteration helped with focus and transmission into the public sphere for what was being done.

Firstly, it was clear that the cathedral would need to receive the human remains. They were in the custody of the University until that point. The 'Reception' followed a day-long journey for King Richard's remains from the Bosworth Battlefield to the City Centre with some short ceremonies and brief prayers at key points along the route. At the cathedral this was to be surrounded in prayer and so the Reception became the first of three public liturgies. These attracted great crowds in the streets, seats in the cathedral were allocated by public ballot and two of the services were televised worldwide. The principal actions on this occasion were that a

The Richard III Reinterment Liturgies

mandate from the Ministry of Justice determining Leicester Cathedral as the final resting place was given to the Dean outside the church. He also took custody of the coffin from the lead archaeologist at the University and this was brought in to the cathedral and placed next to the font.

There then followed the Repose: three full days when the remains, inside their ossuary and coffin and under a pall, sat in repose at the west end of the nave. An estimated 35,000 visitors filed past during that time and the cathedral's pattern of daily prayer and eucharist continued, sometimes involving those who had been a part of the project. This proved to be an unexpected period during which there was an extraordinary display of public spirituality and prayer. Worship that had been planned took on layers of meaning that had increasing depth. Outside the building the railings surrounding the diocesan offices developed a covering of ribbons, each one representing a visitor's prayer. People took purple ribbons to say sorry to God, yellow ribbons for petitions and white ribbons to say thank you. Interestingly the news media simply did not give any attention to this remarkable statement of millions of prayers in the street. Perhaps they did not know what to make of it. Liturgical worship during this period of repose was low-key and simple. For the queues of visitors a specially written prayer from the pulpit led by a chaplain punctuated every half hour. The average wait for people in the queue was four hours.

Inevitably the act of reinterment received the most attention. Leicester Cathedral felt like a very liminal place for the whole week, more so than usual, but there was a strong sense of being on the threshold between mortality and eternity in this act of worship. It is a rare experience in the modern age to inter human remains inside a church building. It is even more unusual for TV cameras to be at a graveside as remains are placed in the ground. Here the whole congregation was at the graveside and the TV audience was drawn there too. The Bishop of Leicester's own daughter had died only a few weeks before the reinterment and he had led the procession to the same place for her funeral. At King Richard's reburial

The Canvas

he preached. This was an intentional choice. There were alternatives and it might have been more natural a decision for the Archbishop of Canterbury to preach. But here a different sort of authority prevailed. The sense of being at the graveside was carried very powerfully.

There was some significant debate about whether there should even be a 'reveal'. But the point here was that there was a story unfolding for the city. The reburial was not the place to notice that. The reburial focused on the life and death of a person, inviting each who participated, in the church or through the medium of television, to reflect on their own personhood. But there was the ongoing and changing life of a city to celebrate. A city that had not been conscious that it had a story now was conscious. This could change how people thought of themselves and their sense of place. And the story of polarity between the houses of Lancaster and York in the fifteenth century contrasted with the story of a multi-cultural city in which there were many more colours than the red and white of the Tudor and Plantagenet roses.

The mass media were not so interested in anything that followed after the reburial rite. The reburial was for them the main event of international importance. Somehow the celebration of a multicultural city at peace with itself whilst being realistic about a history of conflict and polarization was not thought to be as relevant to television viewers as the King's bones being placed back into the ground whence they had come. This lack of interest by the media led to local fears that a final service could fall flat and might be unwise. But there was still a need to open the cathedral to the public somehow after the tomb had been closed (an engineering feat that took most of the night). A liturgy of local celebration using local talent and dramatic symbols was commissioned. It was fully recognized that it would not be possible nor seemly to celebrate even the Easter Gospel during a reburial service. But, if the reburial service was a purple occasion, there needed to be an occasion to wear gold.

The Richard III Reinterment Liturgies

The Structure of the Rites
Having developed an account of what needed to be done in terms of our human transactions there followed the challenge of how to do so properly and authentically within the context of Christian liturgy. The Liturgy Group continued to search for a manual, a model. It so happened that Dr Alexandra Buckle, working in St Anne's College, Oxford, had discovered just such a model in the British Library: an English reinterment liturgy in Latin, actually contemporary with the life of Richard III. The correspondence that followed led to Alexandra joining the Liturgy Group. She tells the story of her discovery and translation and describes this rite in the chapter that follows.

There was something about this 'Latin Rite for the Removal of a Body' that resonated with the needs identified for the reburial in Leicester. It was not just the period in which it had been written down, nor the similarity of its purpose, but rather the way it dealt with liminality. The Latin Rite provided a series of psalms, antiphons, prayers and bible readings, followed by the body being moved being placed in the ground. At this graveside the bishop led prayer and the Benedictus and Lord's Prayer were used. Throughout, the service carried a strong sense of human sinfulness and corruption along with the forgiveness of God mediated by the church. The translation of Joseph's bones from east of the Jordan into the Promised Land is recalled in the Latin service as a warrant for the godliness of moving a person's mortal remains to another place more fitting.

The use of the Benedictus at the graveside is striking. This canticle bears a strong association with the morning through its use historically at this time of day in the Liturgy of the Hours. In the fifteenth century it belonged in the monastic office of Lauds (dawn prayer) and since the sixteenth century it has been the Matins or Morning Prayer Gospel canticle of the Church of England. It is easy to understand why a Gospel song anticipating what God was about to do through the proclamation of John the Baptist's father should be used to signal the beginning of the

The Canvas

day. Here it is applied to the removal and reburial of human remains. So the Latin rite appears to place the reburial into the rhythm of prayers that mark the shape of the day, and within that the morning. It was in the morning when the resurrection was first announced and this rite looks forward to what God is going to do. In a milieu where the Liturgy of the Hours shaped an understanding of the day this is perhaps the most obvious of ways to proceed. To liturgists and cathedral clergy in the present age it made deep sense. For many who would witness the service the resonances may have seemed very thin or non-existent. But conceiving of the reinterment as Morning Prayer was sufficient to give credible and sufficient shape to map the way ahead with deep poesis, historical connection and spiritual depth.

The Latin Rite provided more than plentiful lectionary provision. Fifteenth-century clergy clearly took more time to pray than modern-day TV schedules allow. Channel Four scheduling was undoubtedly a controlling factor for the reburial of King Richard's remains, but it was also an indication of the patience and expectations that many guests would bear. The Liturgy Group limited itself on the whole to material included in the Latin Rite but used the principles outlined in chapter 3 below by Gordon Campbell in editing and adapting the service. The one congregational hymn followed the themes of the Latin Rite ('O God of earth and altar'). The Benedictus was also sung congregationally in metrical form.[3] Contemporary resonance was also carried by Benedict Cumberbatch's reading of poetry by Carol Ann Duffy (he was due to play Richard III in BBC TV's *Hollow Crown*) and music commissioned by Judith Bingham. Three members of the Royal Family were present along with leading nobles from families represented in the Wars of the Roses along with descendants of ordinary people who fought at Bosworth. And Richard III's own Book of Hours was drawn from the Lambeth Palace Library and placed on his coffin whilst in the nave.

---

[3] *Bless the Lord, the God of Israel*, Anne Harrison, sung to *Coverdale*, Maurice Bevan.

Having learned from the medieval church about where the reburial of a person's remains sat within the Liturgy of Hours, we had an opportunity to discover whether the same principles might apply to the Reception and Reveal services.

The contemporary Church of England carries most deeply within its bones the use of Evening Prayer and Night Prayer from the richer and fuller traditions of the Monastic Offices. Although in the Book of Common Prayer Evening Prayer and Compline are combined in Evensong, today they are most familiar as separate services. If the staged rites of the reburial week were to carry any resonance with the patterns of daily prayer then it is to Evening Prayer and Night Prayer that we should look for Reception and Revealing.

It quickly becomes apparent that Compline (Night Prayer) is fundamentally about life and death, the sleep to which the worshippers will shortly be turning being a sign of their deaths to be followed by resurrection. The Compline Gospel Canticle (Nunc Dimittis) looks forward to the grave and this led the group to consider its use for the rite of Reception.

The King's coffin was received in the gardens between the street and the cathedral door and the Dean read words of Job found also in 1 Timothy, 'We brought nothing into the world and we can carry nothing out. The Lord gave, and the Lord has taken away; blessed be the name of the Lord.' The coffin was taken into church and placed before the font where it was asperged with water and covered with a pall. A fifteenth-century Vulgate Bible and a replica crown were placed on the coffin. These acts were reminders of baptism, faith, and the certainty of death irrespective of power and wealth. The office of Compline followed. The only novelties were a motet and a sermon given by the Cardinal Archbishop of Westminster.

Vespers[4] for the Dead undoubtedly has a greater historical precedent

---

[4] Lighting of the lamps, or evening prayer.

The Canvas

than Compline for the Dead. This was an occasion however when the death of the person whose remains were being received had happened so long ago that we had moved a long way from the liminality of the time just before night-fall. The resonances of Compline were very much stronger than any need to light lamps as we might have done around a person who had just slipped into death.

The value of a third great public act of worship during which the cathedral was to be reopened, the tomb revealed and the city's future celebrated had been a moot matter. This idea, however, passed the test of Evensong. The Gospel canticle in this case (Magnificat) is Mary's song of joy for the fulfilment of God's purpose being brought about in her womb. It became a metaphor of a city that would not be the same having made visible its story of the King's end. The shape of prayer through which the church of today hallows the day lent its shape to this week. It was a pattern that seemed complete, and would have been incomplete if the fulfilment belonging to evening had not been celebrated.

The roses were the key. In Plantagenet times the only roses that mattered were red roses and white roses. There is something of this tendency to polarize that infects humanity to the core: Christian or Jew, male or female, white or black, British or immigrant. Leicester stands as the most multicultural city in the UK outside London, and it is not on the whole a polarized place. It feels like a place rich with many coloured roses. And the rose too fits with traditional symbols for Mary whose song is the culmination of Evensong.

The final service became a conversationally structured Service of the Word[5] culminating with the Magnificat. 'Conversations' revolved around Conflict, New Beginnings and New Life followed by an Evening Prayer inspired Conclusion. This was an act of worship to which many guests from the contemporary city were invited and any reliance on Christian heritage was least profitable. Leicester's main theatre company

---

[5] *New Patterns for Worship*, (Church House Publishing, London, 2002) p.19.

provided dance and drama worked through a set that opened up during the service from a World War One landscape to beautiful multi-coloured flower. This was an act of worship that followed contemporary Church of England principles to give structure for world music and dance and visual art and prayer and readings. It celebrated that which God is doing and yet about which people can be so fearful – whether that is fear of death or fear for the future of communities being enriched by others who are different.

2

A medieval starting point:

A unique rite of medieval reburial used in the Church of England in 2015

The document

Deep within the Harley Manuscripts at the British Library is a manuscript that provides a unique source of the late medieval rite of reburial, providing all the directions, prayers, and music to be used. It is a late seventeenth-century copy of a late-fifteenth century manuscript. *BL, MS Harley 6466, ff.33r-34v* is entitled *Ordinacio servicij & observancie pro remocione corporis dicti nuper Comitis* (The Order of Service & Observance for the removal of the body of the foresaid late earl).[6] *Richard' Com Warrwic* (Richard, Earl of Warwick) follows in parentheses. This is because the document was used in conjunction with the reburial of Richard Beauchamp, Earl of Warwick (1382-1439) in his chantry chapel at The Collegiate Church of St Mary, Warwick, in c.1475.[7] However, although the document survives in connection with the reburial of

---

[6] In the margin, it reads, in the same hand, that it was 'Copied out of the Original in the custody of Mr James Fish of Warwick, July 19, 1694'. James Fish was a parish clerk of St Mary's and also looked after the church muniments. See figure 1 overleaf.

[7] I have explored the circumstances of reburial and the dating of this document in "'Entumbid Right Princely": The re-interment of Richard Beauchamp, Earl of Warwick, and a lost rite' in Hannes Kleineke & Christian Steer (Eds), *The Yorkist Age: Proceedings of the 2011 Harlaxton Symposium* (Donington, 2013).

Richard Beauchamp, it details a general rite, with a capital N used where the appropriate name of the reburied could be inserted.

Fig 1: Manuscript BLMS, Harley, 6466, f.33r[8]

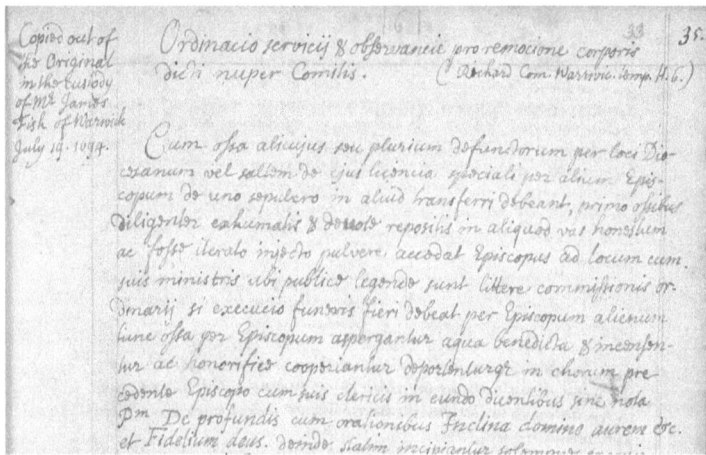

As no other document of medieval reburial is known to survive, this manuscript provides important evidence of the kind of ceremony which may have been used up and down the land at this time. Its creation, within a decade of King Richard III's death, meant it was a valuable source when planning the Leicester reinterment in 2015.

The manuscript, its copyist and its reliability

As has been stated, the manuscript in question is a late-seventeenth century copy of a fifteenth-century copy that no longer survives. As such, it is important to establish its reliability. There is no information given

---

[8] The top two lines of the manuscript provide the title. The small note at the top of the left-hand column indicates when it was copied.

A medieval starting point

regarding the copyist but the Harleian Catalogue in the British Library provides an answer. Number 6466 in this catalogue reads, 'A Quarto, written by Mr Humphrey Wanley', and item six is listed as this reburial rite, as seen in figure 2 below.

Figure 2: the manuscript as quoted in the Harleian Catalogue[9]

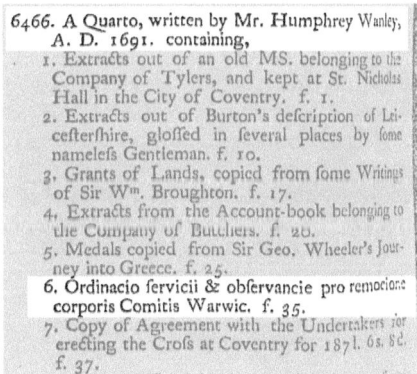

Therefore, the Harleian catalogue provides a name of the copyist. Humphrey Wanley was one of the most respected palaeographers of his day and he has been referred to as 'a great palaeographer'.[10] Wanley held a position as an Assistant Librarian at the Bodleian Library, Oxford, and was involved in compiling Bernard's 1697 well-known *Catalogi Librorum*

---

[9] *A Catalogue of the Harleian Manuscripts in the British Museum* (1808-12), 367. The folio in question is now numbered ff.33r-34v, though it was previously numbered ff.35r-36v.

[10] Neil Ker said that Wanley's 'catalogue of Anglo-Saxon manuscripts is a book which scholars will continue to use, or neglect at their peril': Neil Ripley Ker, *Catalogue of manuscripts containing Anglo-Saxon* (Oxford, 1957), xiii. Wanley's status is also attested in Peter Heyworth, 'Wanley, Humfrey (1672–1726)' in *Oxford Dictionary of National Biography* (first published 2004, accessed online 2016).

Manuscriptorum Anglie at Hiberniae (Catalogue of the Manuscripts in the Libraries of England and Scotland). The reburial rite was included in this catalogue as Item 6703 (22):

A Roll containing the order of the Service and Ceremonies to be used in removing a dead Corps from one Sepulchre to another. This said Roll was written upon the occasion of removing the Body of Richard Beauchamp Earl of Warwick from the place where they has laid it, before the West door of the Chappel of our Lady in the Collegiate Church to the fair Tomb under which it yet remains.[11]

Given Wanley's status, there is little concern about his ability to copy a fifteenth-century scribal hand accurately. It can, therefore, be assumed that this is a reliable copy.

Wanley clearly had a personal interest in this manuscript as he later sent a copy to another established antiquarian, Thomas Tanner (1674–1735). On 28 February 1695, nearly a year after copying Harley MS 6466, Wanley wrote to Tanner, saying 'I sent to Coventry betimes for a Copie of the following service, but my correspondent could not find the MS I di[rect] him to, but as soon as he did, he transcribed it & sent it...'[12] This document survives and is now found in the Bodleian Library (Bodl., MS Tanner 25, f. 309). From 1708 Wanley was employed by Robert Harley (1661–1724) as his librarian and he once again turned to this document, ensuring it had a place in Harley's new library.[13] Since then, Wanley's copy of the manuscript has been forgotten; one may imagine Wanley

---

[11] Edward Bernard and Humfrey Wanley, *Catalogi librorum manuscriptorum Angliæ et Hiberniæ, in unum collecti, cum indice alphabetico* (Oxford, 1697), vol. 2, p. 204.
[12] Bodleian Library, Oxford, MS Tanner 25/2, f. 308; P. L. Heyworth (ed.), *The Letters of Humfrey Wanley. Palaeographer, Anglo-Saxonist, Librarian, 1672–1726. With an Appendix of Documents* (Oxford, 1989), 8. The manuscript was copied on 19 July 1694, see the top-left corner of Figure 1.
[13] This has been explored in greater depth in: Julian Munby, 'Humfrey Wanley and James Fish: the apprentice palaeographer and the lost manuscripts of St Mary's Warwick', *Bodleian Library Record* 25/2 (2012), 217-238.

A medieval starting point

would have been pleased to see it back on the national stage in 2015.

Introducing a medieval reburial ceremony

Very little scholarship has been undertaken on reburial ceremonies. This is, in part, due to the fact that, until the discovery of this manuscript, we did not know what they involved. There are better historical accounts of actual burials and they are more familiar to us today, which means they have had more generous scholarly coverage. In short, a reburial ceremony involved the removal of bones from one tomb to another. Such reburials happened for a number of reasons, including political; familial; prestige and emulation. In some ways a reburial ceremony acted as a type of second funeral: such ceremonies most often occurred ten to thirty years after the funeral itself, which meant that many of the same mourners were present. Principally, the ceremony involved the removal of the body or bones to a more fitting location, either within the same building or to a new location (often to a family mausoleum). Reburial ceremonies were most often organized by family members who were keen to remember their deceased ancestor. Reburial ceremonies said as much about the living as they did about the dead: they brought the deceased into living memory and, at the same time, advertised the status of remaining members of the family.

Putting a reburial ceremony in context

Reburial ceremonies were common at the time Richard III died and had been for some time. The table below shows how important these ceremonies were amongst royalty of the Houses of York and Lancaster. The kings from Richard II to Richard III were each involved with a reburial ceremony, either as its organizer or as a recipient, with the exception of Edward V, and his omission is unsurprising given events surrounding his death.[14]

---

[14] Rosemary Horrox, 'Edward V (1470–1483)', first published 2004; online edition 2013; accessed 2016.

Table 1: Kings associated with reburial ceremonies in the fifteenth century

Name of deceased	Date of death	Place of burial	Date of reburial	Place of reburial	Person behind reburial
Richard II	1400	Kings Langley	1413	Westminster Abbey	Henry V
Richard, Duke of York	1460	Pontefract	1476	St Mary and All Saints, Fotheringhay	Edward IV
Henry VI	1471	Chertsey Abbey	1483	St George's, Windsor	Richard III

Kings were not the only members to be reburied at this time – the Earls of Warwick, Rutland, Suffolk, Somerset, March, Salisbury, Huntingdon, Oxford, Essex and Sussex were also involved, as were the Dukes of York; Norfolk and Clarence. By the close of the fifteenth century, reburial ceremonies had even begun to occur amongst the most aspirational members of the middle classes.

Richard III's father, Richard, Duke of York, is just one example of someone who was reburied. He was killed in battle at Wakefield in 1460 and buried nearby in Pontefract Priory. Sixteen years later his sons arranged for his reburial in the family mausoleum at The Collegiate Church of St Mary and All Saints in Fotheringhay. The nine-day affair is well-documented: full details of the meals consumed, the final feast for more than a thousand people, and how the body was moved, are all covered by the accounts but very little survives regarding the actual reburial ceremony.[15]

---

[15] A. F. Sutton, Livia Visser-Fuchs and P. W. Hammond (eds.), *The Reburial of Richard Duke of York, 21–30 July 1476* (London, 1996).

A medieval starting point

The reburial of Richard III's father is just one example of a common practice amongst the royal and noble élite in the fifteenth century. However, this was not the first time bodies or body parts had been moved in England. The hearts and other body parts of nobles and kings had been moved for at least two centuries before. Important precedents exist in England – the heart, entrails and body of Richard I (1157-1199) were buried in different locations, as were those of Henry I (1068-1135).[16] Heart burial was widespread throughout the twelfth and thirteenth centuries.[17] Similarly, the bodies and remains of saints were often moved. One famous case is the translation of the remains of Thomas Becket in 1220 (buried 1170). This is notable as the liturgies survive from this occasion and are markedly different from the reburial ceremony in question.[18]

What the reburial rite involved

Harley 6466 details the precise way of preparing the bones, and the role of the bishop and other clergy. It also gives full details of the prayers and musical items. The rite is very detailed and so gives a clear picture of what a medieval reburial service involved. The reburial rite alone was a relatively long service with numerous prayers, and musical items. However, this was not the only service that would have taken place on the day. As well as the usual round of daily liturgy, Harley MS 6466 mentions in the first paragraph that, after initial prayers, 'they should immediately begin the solemn exequies for the dead', which included Vespers and Matins of the Dead. The manuscript goes on to state that:

---

[16] Danielle Westerhof, *Death and the Noble Body in England* (Woodbridge, 2008), 82.
[17] Westerhof, *Death and the Noble Body*, 82-83.
[18] The liturgy for Becket was created specifically for him whereas the reburial rite in Harley MS 6466 details a general rite. For more on this, see: Kay Brainerd Slocum, *Liturgies in Honour of Thomas Becket* (Toronto, 2003); Sherry L. Reames, 'Reconstructing and Interpreting a Thirteenth-Century Office for the Translation of Thomas Becket' in *Speculum* 80 (2005), 118-70.

Quibus finitis iterum aspergantur ossa aqua benedicta et sic ibidem remaneant si placet Episcopo usque in crastino post finem misse de Requiem. Sinaliter[19] immediate post dictas exquias sepeliantur precedente Episcopo ad locum [deletions] novi sepulcri cum ossibus...[20]

When these are done, the bones should again be sprinkled with holy water and they should remain there thus, if the Bishop wishes, until the next day after the end of the requiem mass. Otherwise [should the bones not remain there], immediately after having said the exequies, they should be buried, with the Bishop processing to the place of the new tomb with the bones...

Therefore, an option is given to squeeze this into one day or spread it over two days. The tables below show the reburial liturgy that what would have been undertaken on one day or over two days. In total, a reinterment ceremony must have taken several hours to perform.

Table 2: The reburial service on one day

Procession of the bones to the choir
Exequies: Vespers and Matins of the Dead
Procession of the bones
Burial of the bones
Procession
Requiem Mass the following day?

---

[19] This is here corrected. It reads 'Sinantem' in the manuscript.
[20] *BL*, Harley MS 6466, f.33r.

A medieval starting point

Table 3: The reburial service outlined over two days

DAY ONE	DAY TWO
Procession of the bones to the choir	Procession of the bones
Exequies: Vespers and Matins of the Dead	Requiem Mass
	Burial of the bones
	Procession back to the choir

A new rite?

Harley MS 6466 provides a new rite of reburial – no other case is known to survive in medieval Europe. But is the liturgy within it entirely new? Are there any similarities with contemporaneous burial rites? The overall shape of the reburial service in question concurs with burials rites in the *Sarum Manual*, the book containing the texts for priests. A close study of the reburial rite (Harley MS 6466) with the rites of the dead (*Commendatio animarum* and *Inhumatio defuncti*) in fifteenth-century Sarum Manuals shows that many of the prayers, musical items and responses are identical to or variants of those found in the Sarum Manual.[21] However, key differences occur between the Sarum Manual and Harley 6466 to allow for bones rather than a body, and a bishop as celebrant rather than a priest, as the text explicitly states a bishop should perform this rite. At other points, there are significant omissions or re-ordering. An example of such a change can be seen in the prayer, *Obsecramus misericordiam tuam omnipotens*. This has an added section, which refers to how the bones of Joseph were brought from Egypt to Canaan, as outlined in Genesis 50.25, Exodus 13.19 and Joshua 24.32.

---

[21] This is similar to two fifteenth-century Manuals of Sarum Use: Cambridge University Library, Mm. I. 15, and Gonville and Caius College Library, MS 209/115. It is also similar to the printed Sarum Manual: A. J. Collins, ed. *Manuale ad usum percelebris eecclesiae Sarisburiensis*, Henry Bradshaw Society 91 (1960).

The changes made to the prayer in the reinterment rite are shown in bold:

Harley 6466, f.33v: Obsecramus misericordiam tuam omnipotens eterne deus qui hominem ad ymaginem tuam creare dignatus es quique; ***ossa sanctissimi Joseph per filios Israel in eorum exitu de Egipto ad terram promissionis deferri voluisti*** ut anima famuli tui N cujus ***ossa*** hodierna die ***ad novum transferrimus mausoleum*** blande et misericorditer suscipias non ei dominetur umbra mortis nec tegat eum chaos et caligo tenebrarum sed exuta omnium criminum labe et in sinum Abrahe collocata locum refrigerij se adeptam esse gaudeat ut cum dies judicij advenerit cum sanctis et electis tuis eam [sic] ***redempto corpore*** jubeas ***collocari sine fine*** per Christum Dominum nostrum. Amen.[22]

Sarum Manual: Obsecramus misericordiam tuam omnipotens eterne deus qui hominem ad imaginem tuam creare dignatus es: **[section added about Joseph and his bones in the reburial rite]** ut animam famuli tui vel famule tue N. quam hodierna die ***rebus humanis eximi et ad te accersiri iussisti*** blande et misericorditer suscipias. Non ei dominentur umbre mortis: nec tegat eum *vel* eam chaos et caligo tenebrarum: sed exutus *vel* exuta omnium criminum labe in sinu Abrahe collocatus *vel* collocata/ locum refrigerij se adeptum *vel* adeptam esse gaudeat: ut cum dies judicij advenerit/ cum sanctis et electis tuis eum vel eam ***resuscitari*** jubeas. Per Christum Dominum nostrum. Amen.[23]

---

[22] This prayer includes several gendered oddities. Masculine pronouns are given throughout the rite apart from in two prayers where feminine pronouns are given – this is one of them. Sarum Manuals often give two alternatives in the rite for the burial of the dead – for both the masculine and feminine (eg exuta/exutus or eam/eum) but here in BLMS Harley 6466 mistakes are made. This may tell us vital information about the source from which this was copied but this is the subject for another paper.

[23] Collins, *Manuale ad usum percelebris eecclesiae Sarisburiensis*, 156.

A medieval starting point

English translation of Harley 6466, f.33r: Let us pray. We beseech your mercy, omnipotent eternal God, who have deigned to create man in your image *and who wished the bones of the most holy Joseph to be carried away by the children of Israel in their exodus from Egypt to the promised land, that you kindly and* mercifully take up the soul of your servant N. [INSERT NAME], *whose bones we transfer today to a new tomb*, so that the shade of death not control him nor chaos and the darkness of shadows cover him, but, released from the defect of all sins and placed in the bosom of Abraham, he may rejoice to have arrived at a place of refreshment, so that when the day of judgement comes, you may ordain his soul, *rejoined to his body*, to be placed with your saints and chosen ones for ever. Through Christ our Lord. Amen.

It is clear why such a prayer was altered in a rite dealing with bones. There is also a new prayer in the rite, not known to exist in any other liturgy. This new prayer also draws on bones but this time from the famous biblical passage about Ezekiel's vision of bones in Ezek.37. Both prayers were clearly devised with a reburial ceremony in mind: they make careful use of passages from the bible relating to bones. These two prayers were retained for the reinterment of King Richard III and they will be discussed below.

Adapting the rite for 2015
We were faced with a number of issues when adapting this two-day medieval service into a modern-day, fifty-minute service of national importance. Our process involved tailoring the medieval rite to one appropriate for the Church of England in 2015 and, thereby, cutting and pruning this long service but retaining intelligibility. Simultaneously, we had to add items to aid comprehensibility. Modern points of orientation also had to be inserted, such as hymns, a sermon and the national anthem.

I shall discuss omissions from the medieval rite first. Some prayers had to be omitted because of their length; others because of inappropriate sentiment. An example of a prayer, which was removed from the original reburial rite for March 2015 is given below:

Deus vite dator & humanorum corporum reparator qui te a peccatoribus exorari voluisti exaudi preces quas speciali devocione pro anima famuli tui N tibi[24] *lacrimabiliter fundimus ut liberare eam ab inferorum cruciatibus & collocare inter agmina sanctorum tuorum digneris. veste quoq; celesti & stola immortalitatis indui & paradisi amenitate jubeas confoveri*[25] *per Christum.*[26]

Lord, giver of life and repairer of those human bodies, who have wished to be entreated by sinners, hear those prayers which we tearfully pour out to you in special devotion for the soul of your servant N [INSERT NAME], that you deign to free it [eam, the soul] from the torments of those below and place him among the host of your saints. Also clothe him in a heavenly garment and the stole of immortality and command him to be fostered in the pleasantness of paradise. Through Christ our Lord. Amen.

This prayer discusses the 'torments of those below', whilst others graphically described 'the filthy whirlpool of this world'. These highly evocative descriptions are sentiments from a different age and were not deemed to be appropriate for a service in the Church of England in 2015. Additionally, this prayer and others that were omitted use the word 'tearfully' ('lacrimabiliter'). Reburial services carried out within ten to thirty years of death would have invited mourning amongst the

---

[24] This appears as 'tibi que' in the manuscript.
[25] This appears as 'consoneri' in the manuscript, with a mark over the letter *n* to indicate a doubt on the part of the transcriber (Ware;e. I am grateful to John Caldwell for help in transcribing this.
[26] *BL*, Harley MS 6466, f.34r.

A medieval starting point

attendees; such sadness would have been entirely fitting. However, the five-hundred-year gap between the present day and Richard III's death meant that any personal connection with the deceased was removed and, therefore, such language was not appropriate. Here, the focus turned to that of dignity and respect. Other prayers had to be changed to adopt a more modern language and not a straight translation from the Latin. An example of a prayer that was adapted is the unique prayer discussing Ezekiel's bones, discussed earlier. Below, the Latin is given from the rite, as well as an English translation and then the adapted prayer, as it appeared in the Order of Reinterment for Richard III.

Straight transcription from Latin in BL, Harley MS 6466, f.33r: Omnipotens sempiterne Deus animarum conditor & redemptor qui per Ezechielis vaticinium ossa vehementer arida nervis compi[n]gere pelle & carnibus superinduere ac in ea spiraculum vite intromittere dignatus es : te supplices deprecamur pro anima[27] cari nostri N cujus ossa jam denuo tradimus sepultur[a] ut ei tribuere digneris placidam & quietam mansionem & remittas omnes lubrice temeritatis offensas ut concessa sibi venia plene indulgentie quicquid in hoc seculo proprio vel alieno reatu deliquit totum ineffabili pietate tua deleas & abstergas Qui cum deo patre et spiritu sancto unus.

English translation from Latin: Let us pray. Omnipotent and eternal God, creator and redeemer of souls, who through the prophecy of Ezekiel are worthy to bind together truly dry bones with sinews, to cover them with skin and flesh, and to put into them the breath of life, we supplicants pray to you for the soul of our dear N [INSERT NAME] whose bones we now place in the grave that you may deign to grant him a peaceful and quiet resting place and, that having remitted all his sins of worldly heedlessness as conceded to him by a pardon

---

[27] Should be 'animam'.

of full indulgence, that, through your ineffable mercy, you erase and wash away all of it, whatever he has erred in this world by his own or another's guilt. Who with God the Father and the Holy Spirit lives and reigns, God through all for ever and ever. Amen.

Changed for the Order of Reinterment: Almighty and eternal God, creator and redeemer of souls, who by the prophecy of Ezekiel considereth it worthy to bind together truly dry bones with sinews, to cover them with skin and flesh, and to put into them the breath of life: as we return the bones of thy servant Richard to the grave, we beseech thee to grant him a peaceful and quiet resting place, through Jesus Christ our Lord, who liveth and reigneth with God the Father in the unity of the Holy Ghost, one God, world without end. Amen.

Sourcing the music

There is not any musical notation in Harley MS 6466 but it does list the title of musical works, and from these they were easily sourced. For example, an antiphon is listed as '*A. In Paradisum*' and a Psalm as '*Ps. In exitu Israel*'. From these titles, the musical items were easily obtained from other liturgical books of chant. In total, Harley MS 6466 calls for six antiphons and seven psalms, with all but one being sung.

Harley MS 6466 stipulates a bishop must act as the celebrant, which limited the books of chant that could be used to source the music as most chant sources appear in books used by priests (e.g. the manual). There are very few bishop's books (pontificals), which include notation from this time. Two significant pontificals survive with music. One originates from the Coventry and Lichfield diocese, and dates to the fourteenth century.[28] However, it does not include chants from the rites of burial and so was not suitable. The Bangor Pontifical is the other option. Although the Bangor pontifical was copied in the early fourteenth century, probably

---

[28] *Cul*, MS Ff.6.9.

A medieval starting point

during the bishopric of Anian II, Bishop of St Asaph, Bangor (d.1305-7), there is evidence that it was still being used by the bishop in Bangor in 1465-94 (Richard Ednam), and therefore at the same time as Harley MS 6466 was compiled and during Richard III's lifetime.[29]

Figure 3: Bangor Pontifical

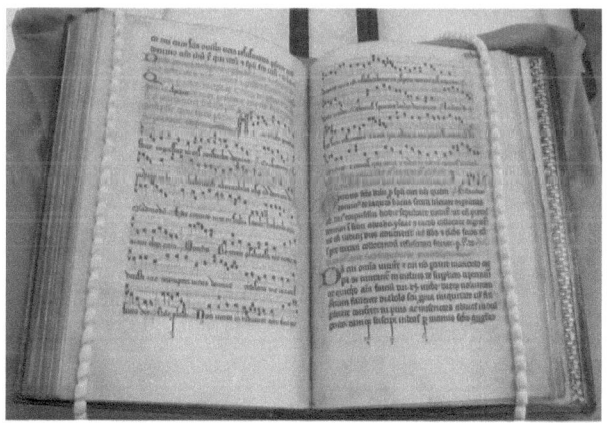

The Bangor Pontifical is of the Use of Salisbury and contains all of the antiphons listed in Harley MS 6466 (see below). The antiphons taken from the Bangor Pontifical closely relate to those in the Sarum Manual.[30]

---

[29] Sally Harper, 'The Bangor Pontifical: a Pontifical of the Use of Salisbury' in *Welsh Music History* 2 (1997), 66. The most detailed study of the Bangor Pontifical has been undertaken by Sally Harper, *Music in Welsh Culture before 1650* (Ashgate, Aldershot, 2007), 238. It contains two rites which feature the same choral items as described in Harley MS 6466: the last rites ('Ordo ad sepeliendum corpus',) and the carrying of a body to the church ('Cum portatur corpus ad ecclesiam'). The second rite (Cum portatur) was here found to correspond closely with the *Sarum Manual*.

[30] Harper, 'The Bangor Pontifical', 82. The close correspondence between these items in the Bangor Pontifical and those in the Sarum Manual will be the subject of a forthcoming paper.

The Richard III Reinterment Liturgies

Table 4: Harley and Bangor musical items

Lbl, Harley MS 6466, ff.33r-34v	Bangor Pontifical: *Cum portatur corpus ad ecclesiam*
De profundis (Ps) this is spoken at Warwick and not sung	f.158r
In Paradisum (A)	f.158r
In exitu Israel (Ps)	Not included
Aperite (A)	f.160r
Confitemini (Ps)	f.160r
Ingrediar (A)	f.160v
Quemadmodum (Ps)	f.160v
De terra (A)	f.161v
Domine probasti (Ps)	f.161v
Omnis Spiritus (A)	f.162r
Laudate (Ps)	f.162r
Ego sum (A)	f.162r
Benedictus (Canticle)	f.162r

Some of these musical items had to be removed for the reinterment of Richard III because of their length. Three psalms were retained and three of the six antiphons were sung in the service along with the Benedictus (which became a hymn) and Ego sum, which was spoken as the Dismissal ('I am the resurrection and the life. Those who believe in me, even though they die, will live, and everyone who lives and believes in me will never die'). Of the three antiphons, two remained as they appear in the Bangor Pontifical and the other was incorporated into a piece by Philip Moore, as can be seen below.

A medieval starting point

Table 5: Musical items used in the 2015 reburial service from Harley MS 6466

Musical Item in Harley 6466	Music used in service for Reinterment of Richard III
Psalm 150 Antiphon: *Omnis spiritus*	By Philip Moore This, as appears in the Bangor Pontifical, was incorporated into Moore's setting
Psalm 138 Antiphon: *De terra*	Verses from Psalm 138 set to a piece by 15th-century composer Leonel Power (motet, Beata progenies). This was sung as presented in the Bangor Pontifical
Psalm 114 Antiphon: *In Paradisum*	This was reconstructed for the occasion This was sung as presented in the Bangor Pontifical

As is evident, Harley MS 6466 guided the selection of music. Other items were included that were not taken from the reburial rite, such as a newly-commissioned anthem by Judith Bingham. The inclusion of such items are an expectation in services of this nature.

Conclusion

Harley MS 6466 contains an interesting mix of familiar and non-familiar elements: there are prayers still used regularly today such as the Lord's Prayer and the committal, 'earth to earth, ashes to ashes, dust to dust'. However, there are also unique prayers – prayers that do not appear in any other liturgy. The medieval rite of reburial is interesting in being an entirely new piece of liturgy and yet one that simultaneously borrows from contemporaneous burial rites. As has been shown, it is closely related to medieval rites of burial as found in the Sarum Manual yet significant features separate it from the usual burial service.

The Richard III Reinterment Liturgies

The rediscovery of this rite, just a few years before the remains of Richard III were found, meant that this document answered a number of questions about how to rebury a king: it provided a Catholic rite, an 'authentic' medieval rite and it permitted its own adaptation by way of its implicit flexibility. There is something cyclical about the borrowing and adaptation of an existing liturgy for a new purpose: just as this medieval reburial rite was borrowed from an existing liturgy and transformed in the fifteenth century; more recently, in 2015, five hundred years later, it was modified once again. This manifests a profound timelessness to this extraordinary piece of liturgy; a piece whose surprising contemporary relevance has only very recently been revealed.

3

The Language of Liturgy in two ages

Richard III was the last English king to die in battle. When his bones were recovered in 2012, they became the subject of a legal battle, this time without bloodshed, but nonetheless fought with high passion. When it was finally decided that the bones should be buried in Leicester Cathedral, yet another battle broke out, this time about the nature of the services that were appropriate to the re-interment of a medieval king. Some thought that King Richard should have a Catholic burial; others favoured a traditional Anglican ceremony; still others thought that a multi-faith ceremony would be appropriate. Within the archaeological community, some thought that he should not be reinterred at all, because new knowledge could be generated by new technology if the bones were to remain available for analysis for the indefinite future; others thought that as a usurper and a child-killer, King Richard did not deserve a Christian burial.

The notion that Richard was a usurper and a child-killer is contested. David Horspool, Richard's most recent scholarly biographer, argues in *Richard III: a ruler and his reputation* (2015) that Richard was simply a man of his times, albeit nasty times, and considers that Richard did indeed murder his rivals, including the princes in the Tower. He concludes that 'whether or not Richard was a bad man, he was a bad king'. This sensible view, which is built on a solid scholarly foundation, is contested by members of the Richard III Society, who portray Richard as a saintly figure and a compassionate king who ruled in the interests of his people. Academics may roll their eyes at such views, but the opinion was formed at Leicester Cathedral that the Church should welcome all comers, and so must accommodate those whose views are far removed from the scholarly consensus. Ricardians were therefore welcome at the table of the liturgical feast, made their mark on the composition of the liturgies, and in the event attended the services in large numbers as well as organizing a service of their own, are for which the appointed Liturgy Group bore no responsibility.

The Liturgy Group's three principal services did not embody or articulate a moral view of Richard as a man or as a king. We were interring an anointed king of England, a faithful member of the Church, with the honour and dignity that he had been denied when he was first buried. Some have queried our insistence on Richard's well-documented piety on the grounds that he murdered his way to the throne, but our view was that faith and sin have never been mutually exclusive, and it is possible that Richard saw his butchery as a divinely-sanctioned path to a throne that God had destined for him. It is hard enough to understand the thinking of our own parents, much less the thinking of a fifteenth-century king, and we chose to set aside Richard's motives as unknowable, and instead focus on his standing as a king anointed in the name of God.

Members of the public who wrote letters to the press and to the cathedral advocating or demanding a Catholic burial did so on the grounds that Richard had died a Catholic and should therefore be given a Catholic funeral. Some argued that the services should be in Latin. The first of these contentions assumes that the successor of the *ecclesia anglicana* of which King Richard was a member is the Roman Catholic church, and that the present Church of England is a breakaway occasioned by Henry VIII's passions being aroused by Anne Boleyn. We were inclined to resist this view, noting that Henry VIII continued to regard himself as Catholic, and arguing that the Church of England is the successor of Richard's *ecclesia anglicana*. Indeed, King Henry destroyed the monastic establishment in England, but left the cathedrals largely unreformed, so within the cathedrals the rhythms of the canonical hours

The Language of Liturgy in two ages

continued to be observed. The services that we devised for our cathedral were incorporated into those hours.

The argument posed for Latin was based on the assumption that services should be held in a language that no-one understands. In fact, the liturgy of the church has been conducted in local languages since the days of the primitive church. The earliest rituals were conducted in Aramaic, and in late antiquity the eucharist was celebrated in languages such as Syriac and Coptic. In the eastern Mediterranean the common language was Greek, and so the celebration was in Greek. When Latin began to replace Greek, liturgies were often a hybrid of Greek and Latin; the Kyrie at the beginning of the Latin mass is a vestige of that earlier tradition. At the time of Richard III, Latin was the language of educated people in England, in schools and universities, for example, the spoken language was Latin. The shift from Latin to the vernaculars was as gradual as the earlier shift from Greek to Latin: Protestants abandoned it in the liturgy (though not in theological writing) in the sixteenth century, and Catholics followed suit at the Second Vatican Council. We resolved to write in English, but just as the Kyrie is a reminder of a superseded language, so the eulogist at the re-interment service concluded, at the behest of the Dean, with the phrase *requiescat in pace*, pronounced as late ecclesiastical Latin. Latin was also used in some of the music in each of the services.

The Liturgy Group had to bear all these sentiments in mind when creating the services. There was, however, a larger and more important constituency to be considered: we were not writing to satisfy the conflicting demands of the special interest groups that pressed us from every quarter, but rather for the congregations gathered within the cathedral, and for the millions of ordinary people who would watch the first two ceremonies on television. The dynamic of the occasion would be established by the fortunate few who were present in the cathedral for each of the services, and we were conscious that these were largely unchurched congregations, and so would be unfamiliar with the rites of the Church of England. In prayer, for example, clergy assumed the orans posture (depicted in the orders of service in the form of the cathedral's logo), but we did not suggest that members of the congregations kneel in prayer, as such in-house practices could have discomfited some of those in attendance. We also realized that we could not exploit one of the most powerful resources of liturgy, which is familiarity with repeated words and indeed repeated services.

In this complex cultural context, it was important to choose an appropriate language for our liturgy. There was a rightful insistence that our language be communicative, which meant that we could not luxuriate in the archaic language that can offer the comfort of familiarity to practising Anglicans. Such archaisms may survive in Christmas carols, which means most of those singing 'O come all ye faithful' will have no idea what 'Very God' means (or think that it means something like 'very last century'), or what distinction is implied in 'begotten not created', but such recondite language could have no place in our services. On the other hand, we were burying an anointed king in an Anglican cathedral, so there was no need for us to cultivate the illusion of spontaneity with *ex tempore* prayers. We could neither forfeit our link to the centuries of liturgy that lay behind our services, nor could we create a language that sounded false either to traditionalists or to those imprisoned in the language of the present.

What language is appropriate to liturgy? Just as in court one addresses the bench in formal and traditional terms (judges are not addressed by their first names), so in addressing God in the liturgy, we use formal terms of address. Prayers are not addressed to Jesus of Nazareth, but to our Lord and Saviour Jesus Christ. Often the prayer contains a vocative 'O', so the Dean's opening prayer (on which more below) at the Reinterment Service began 'Hear our prayers, O Lord'. Such forms of address are typical of the linguistic register of liturgical language, and rightly so. They are mildly archaic, but they are readily understood. Indeed, we eschewed any language that would merely bemuse the listener. We might, for

The Language of Liturgy in two ages

example, in a spirit of ecumenical outreach spanning the centuries, have contemplated using the Lord's Prayer in the Douay-Rheims translation. Had we done so, our congregation would have said 'Give us this day our supersubstantial bread'. Scholars might have nodded with respect to the rendering of the *hapax legomenon epiousios*, and felt a little superior to those who had been gulled by the Vetus Latina assertion (*panem nostrum quotidianum da nobis hodie*) into thinking of the bread as 'daily', but we were not in the business of making scholars feel smug: our language was formal, but at every point was meant to be understood. The Dean's opening prayer went on to say 'as we beseech you', which is ecclesiastical English, but it is widely understood, and avoids the archaism of 'thee', which was sparingly used in these services. The same prayer ends with 'Amen'. Some would have us translate this Hebrew term (perhaps as 'certainly' or 'absolutely' or 'yes, yes, yes'), but the liturgical link to the affirmation of the prayer that it concludes would have been lost. Here as in countless other instances, we chose the via media.

The liturgy of the service of reinterment posed an additional challenge, because it was modelled on the fifteenth-century reburial service discovered by Dr Alexandra Buckle, and that service was in Latin. Indeed, some thought that the entire service should be in pre-Tridentine Latin, perhaps according to the Sarum Use or even the Use of Lincoln. The argument for the Sarum Use is that by the mid-fifteenth century it was in near-universal use in England, and King Richard specified its use in the statutes of the College of Middleham. The argument for the Lincoln Rite is that Leicester was for many centuries, including the fifteenth, in the diocese of Lincoln, and that it was this rite (mentioned by Cranmer in his preface to the 1549 Book of Common Prayer) that would have been in use in Leicester at the time of Richard's burial. The practical impediment to using this rite is that apart from a few pages preserved in the Bodleian, the Lincoln Rite is lost.

The supervening argument, however, is that ours was not a funeral, but rather a reburial. We assume that the Franciscan friars prayed when they buried Richard and remembered him in mass the next morning. These two occasions, in our view, constituted a funeral. We were not burying a king, but rather reburying one, so we needed a reburial service. There were many reburials in fifteenth-century England, but until Dr Buckle found the one that we were to adapt to our purposes, there was no evidence of the texts around which services were built.

The Liturgy Group was responsible for three services. The reception of the remains of King Richard into the cathedral took the form of a service of Compline that inaugurated a canonical cycle of Morning Prayer, Evening Prayer and daily Eucharist. We followed the form of the reburial rites with which King Richard would have been familiar, in that reception at Compline was followed by a reinterment service based on Mattins, and later by a concluding service that was in essence an elaboration of Vespers.

The rite of Compline was absorbed into Evensong in the Book of Common Prayer in 1549, 1559 and 1662, but in the revision of 1928 a form of Compline was reintroduced as a separate service *'when Evensong has been previously said'*. In the Roman Catholic Church, Compline has an unbroken history that extends from the Rule of St Benedict (or earlier) up to the present, so our choice of Compline lent towards the tradition of the church King Richard knew and to the confessional sensibility of our principal guest, His Eminence Cardinal Vincent Nichols, who censed the coffin, preached the sermon and led the Collect. A further acknowledgement of the Roman Catholic tradition was the recessional, *Ave Regina Caelorum*, which was based on a Marian Antiphon for the season of Lent. Prayers were taken from versions of the Prayer Book that retain 'thee' and 'thou' (e.g. ' Grant, Lord, that we who are baptised into the death of thy Son our Saviour Jesus Christ may continually put to death our evil desires'), archaic 'shew' ('O Lord, shew thy mercy upon us') and '-eth' third-person inflections ('who liveth and reigneth with thee'). The principal innovation in this service was the Collect from the statutes of Middleham College (founded by King Richard in 1478)

The Language of Liturgy in two ages

which was to have been recited daily by the clergy of the College after the King had died. This was the rogation supplication *Deus cui proprium est misereri semper et parcere*. Rather than translate it afresh, we took advantage of its presence in the Book of Common Prayer, and used the 1928 text.

The principal service, by the measure of VIPs in attendance rather than liturgical significance, was the reinterment service. It was this service that was modelled on the reburial service that Dr Buckle had discovered. In it was embedded the story of the bones of Joseph, which offered some instructive parallels to the story of the bones of the person whose remains were to be interred, in this case King Richard. Co-incidentally, we know that at the time of Joseph, 'the sojourning of the children of Israel, who dwelt in Egypt, was four hundred and thirty years' (Exodus 12.40). If we allow for 40 years in the wilderness, during which the bones were guarded by the Israelites, then the period in question is almost five centuries, and for most of that period we do not know where the bones were guarded. King Richard died in 1485, and for more than five centuries we did not know where his bones were buried.

Joseph was eventually buried in Shechem, on the outskirts of what is now the city of Nablus, in the West Bank. His tomb is a site of pilgrimage for Christians, Jews, Muslims and Samaritans. Leicester is a city that happily accommodates Christians, Jews, and Muslims, as well as many good Samaritans. The central theme of the story of the bones of Joseph is promise and fulfilment. As Hebrews 11.22 explains, 'By faith Joseph, when he died, made mention of the departing of the children of Israel, and gave commandment concerning his bones'. Joseph's commandment reflected his faith, and the removal of the bones signified the intention of the Israelites never to return to bondage. The story underlined the appropriateness of a dignified burial in a setting appropriate to the faith of Joseph.

The service began with the eulogy, which was not part of the liturgy, followed by the opening prayer, the procession and a hymn. The opening prayer was a version of our fifteenth-century text, which was borrowed from the burial rites in the Use of Sarum.

Inclina, Domine, aurem tuam ad preces nostras, quibus misericordiam tuam supplices deprecamus, ut animam famuli tui, quam de hoc saeculo migrare jussisti, in pacis ac lucis regione constituas et sanctorum tuorum jubeas esse consortem. Per Dominum nostrum Jesum Christum Filium tuum, qui tecum vivit et regnat in unitate Spiritus Sancti, Deus per omnia saecula saeculurum. Amen.

Here our prayers, O Lord, as we beseech you to have mercy upon the souls of your servants whom you have commanded to pass out of this world. Draw them into the realm of light and peace, and welcome them to be among your faithful departed through Christ our Lord, who is alive and reigns with you in the unity of the Holy Spirit, one God, now and for ever. Amen

The difficulty is that the prayer contains prayers for the dead, a Roman Catholic doctrine that has not always fared well in the Church of England. It lived on very briefly at the Reformation, but was denounced in 1547 in Cranmer's Homily on Prayer and was deleted entirely from the 1552 Book of Common Prayer. There were attempts to reinstate such prayers in the proposed 1928 Book, and at present the position seems to be principled ambiguity. At Princess Diana's funeral, the Dean of Westminster said 'we entrust you to God', and on the tenth anniversary of her death the Archbishop of Canterbury said 'May she rest in peace where sorrow and pain are banished, and may the everlasting light of your merciful love shine upon her'. Archbishop Rowan's 'may' hovers delicately on a fulcrum capable of tilting either towards an expression of hope or towards the petitioning of God. Dr Williams is extraordinarily adept in the use of language that is inclusive in the sense of embracing a wide range of confessional sensibilities. We took such examples to be

The Language of Liturgy in two ages

permissive, and in our translation endeavoured to proffer comfort to any who care about this recondite theological question, as well as to the large number of people who have never noticed that such a question exists. That is why 'we beseech you' leans in its slightly archaic phrasing towards the idea of petition, whereas phrases that might seem at first glance to be instructing God ('draw them . . . welcome them') are in fact expressions of hope.

The Dean's greeting that followed included the first of the readings appropriate to Joseph (Genesis 50.25), followed by the Lord's Prayer, not in the traditional version of 1662 ('which art in heaven') nor in a contemporary version such as *The Message* ('Our Father in heaven, Reveal who you are. Set the world right; Do what's best'), but in the slightly archaic 1928 version ('Our Father who art in heaven').

Next followed the Collect, where the serious challenges lay. The fifteenth-century text from which we worked had three sections, which we divided into three sentences:

Obsecramus misericordiam tuam omnipotens eterne deus qui hominem ad ymaginem tuam creare dignatus es quiq; ossa sanctissimi Joseph per filios Israel in eorum exitu de Egipto ad terram promissionis deferri voluisti ut anima famuli tui N cujus ossa hodierna die ad novum transferrimus mausoleum.

We implore your mercy, almighty and eternal God who saw fit to create humankind in your image and who desired that the bones of Joseph be carried away by the children of Israel in their journey from Egypt to the promised land. Kindly and mercifully receive us with your servant Richard, whose bones we transfer to a new tomb today.

The 'N' in the Latin is *nomen*, and we chose simply to insert the name 'Richard', stripped of his regal title. Whatever our station in life, we are in death all deemed to be sinners in need of redemption. We quietly omitted to translate *sanctissimi* lest it frighten the Protestant horses, and we risked the gender-neutral 'humankind', as we had no wish to promote patriarchy. We also chose to transfer rather than translate the bones, and in this instance we had the Latin on our side.

Blande et misericorditer suscipias non ei dominetur umbra mortis nec tegat eum chaos & caligo tenebrarum sed exuta omnium criminum labe et in sinum Abrahe.

May the shadow of death not govern us nor chaos and darkness consume us, but, cleansed from the stains of all sin, may we be gathered at a place of refreshment in the bosom of Abraham.

The choice of archaic 'cleansed' obliterated the possibility of any distracted thoughts of washing machines removing stains. The most difficult issue was the reference to the bosom of Abraham. Pedants would know that the expression arises in the parable of Dives and Lazarus, and refers to the practice (observed in Roman Palestine) of dining in the *triclinium* not in a seated posture but rather reclining on the chest of one's fellow diners. Jesus means that Lazarus will recline on Abraham at the heavenly feast. The translation hinted at this sense in the phrase 'place of refreshment'. We allowed the phrase itself to stand (instead of 'the abode of the righteous dead') because it is familiar to many beyond the church through 'Rock my soul' and though literary references (Wordsworth's 'It is a beauteous evening' has 'Thou liest in Abraham's bosom all the year') and familiar plays (in Shakespeare's *Henry V*, Mistress Quickly says 'He's in Arthur's bosom, if ever man went to Arthur's bosom'). The confusion of Arthur and Abraham implies a sixteenth-century audience sufficiently familiar with both to see the joke.

Our original read:

Collocata locum refrigerij se adeptam esse gaudeat ut cum dies judicij

The Language of Liturgy in two ages

advenerit cum sanctis et electis tuis eam redempto corpore jubeas collocari sine fine per Christum Dominum nostrum. Amen.
But we redrafted it as:

When the day of judgement comes, gather us together with Richard and all your saints and all the faithful departed forever through Jesus Christ our Lord who is alive and reigns with you in the unity of the Holy Spirit one God, for ever and ever. Amen.

The real difficulty lay in the phrase *cum sanctis et electis tuis*. It was clear that 'sanctis' referred to saints in the Roman Catholic sense of the word (those who have been canonized) rather than the Protestant sense (as in 'When the saints go marching in'), so the simplest solution was simply to let the term stand in all its shimmering ambiguity. But what did the term 'elect' mean in the century before Calvin? The advice of learned Catholic friends, was that the Thomist sense of election as an act of divine will that preceded predestination had not achieved any consensus, and that the precise understanding of the term in fifteenth-century England probably lay beyond recovery. We therefore, following Anglican liturgical advice, chose to deploy the phrase 'faithful departed', which helpfully encompasses a broad range of meanings.

The prayers of the reinterment spoken by the Archbishop of Canterbury again drew on the fifteenth-century service, in which the prayer was:

Omnipotens sempiterne Deus, animarum conditor et redemptor, qui per Ezechielis vaticinium ossa vehementer arida nervis compingere, pelle et carnibus superinduere, ac in ea spiraculum vitæ intromittere dignatus es: te supplices deprecamur pro anima in cari nostri N cuius ossa iam denuo tradimus sepultura, ut ei tribuere digneris placidam et quietam mansionem et remittas omnes lubrice temeritatis offensas, ut concessa sibi venia plenæ indulgentiæ quicquid in hoc seculo proprio vel alieno reatu deliquit, totum ineffabili pietate tua deleas et abstergas. Qui cum Deo Patre et Spiritu Sancto vivis et regnas, Deus per omnia sæcula sæculorum. Amen.

Here we redrafted:

Almighty and eternal God, creator and redeemer of souls, who by the prophecy of Ezekiel deigned to bind together dry bones with sinews, to cover them with skin and flesh, and to put into them the breath of life: as we return the bones of your servant Richard to the grave, we beseech you to grant him a peaceful and quiet resting place, through Jesus Christ our Lord, who is alive and reigns with you, in the unity of the Holy Spirit, one God, for ever and ever. Amen.

The most remarkable – some would say reprehensible – feature of our translations was what we left out. We were shortening a very long service, but the choice of what to cut was ours, and in this instance we chose to pass over the words that might be translated:

having received the remission of sins of worldly carelessness through a pardon of full indulgence, we ask that through your ineffable mercy, you erase and wash away all of his sins, however he has erred in this world by his own or another's guilt.

Leo X's sale of indulgences served the admirable cause of raising money to complete St Peter's, but it irked a German friar, and we still live with the consequences of the schism that followed. As our purposes included the fostering of reconciliation between Catholics and Protestants witnessing our services, it would have been pointlessly divisive to raise the issue, so we quietly omitted it.

Such radical change in our version of the fifteenth-century text that we inherited was no accident. Ours was not an antiquarian recreation,

The Language of Liturgy in two ages

but rather an attempt to adapt a rite that in its original form would not have allowed a twenty-first century congregation to understand or pray. The office structure of the original rite suited our modern sensibility admirably, and the narrative of the bones of Joseph had extraordinary resonance in our own time, but the world has changed in the 530 years since Richard's death, and it seemed imperative that we reinterpret the liturgy for the twenty-first century.

The liturgy of the service ended with the Dismissal Gospel read by the Dean, but the presence of members of the royal family made it appropriate that immediately after the service we sing the National Anthem. The text of the Anthem sanctioned by the monarchy consists of two of the original six verses and we chose to sing both, in part because the reference in the second verse to the monarch's duty to defend our laws, admirably achieved by our present Queen, glances back towards the one aspect of King Richard's reign that we might cautiously admire, which is his concern for the rule of law. It is easy to mock the exaggerated claims of Ricardians about the significance of his legal reforms, but David Horspool's cool examination of the evidence demonstrates that at least some of Richard's innovations seem to have been motivated by a desire to improve the lives of his subjects. The National Anthem may have been liturgically separate from the service, but it served to underline a positive aspect of the reign of the King over whose burial we had just presided.

The last of the three services centred around the revealing of the tomb. Drama was introduced into the ritual of the Church in the tenth century with the enactment of the *Visitatio sepulchri* (visit to the tomb) in a liturgical dialogue known by its opening phrase as *Quem quaeritis* (whom do you seek?), the question of the angel to the Marys. We commissioned Curve Theatre Leicester to produce a theatrical revelation of King Richard's tomb. The echo of the tomb of Jesus was an unspoken reminder of the link between the tomb and the resurrection, a link made more explicit in the responsory at the end of the service, when the resurrection is linked to 'the firstfruits of those who have fallen asleep'.

The Richard III Reinterment Liturgies

The service had a strong civic dimension, in that the tomb was being revealed to the city and the county – not to the wider world, as there was no television coverage. Leicester is a multi-faith city, and the presence of visitors from the various communities made it imperative that the language of the service be accessible to all. The three dramatic performances by Curve accomplished this objective brilliantly, and the liturgy group's task was to ensure that our part in the service was similarly accessible. The conception of Curve's performance was secular, though the music performed during the dramatic sequences was sacred. Our challenge was to ensure that the liturgical elements were Christian but not partisan. The three lessons were read by people associated with the city, the county and Curve Theatre, and were all taken from the Old Testament. Similarly, no prayer mentioned Jesus. Instead, Christian elements appeared in the music performed by the choir, in clerical words directed towards the congregation (such as the Blessing and the Dismissal) and in one of the hymns – non-Christians are usually comfortable with singing Christian music, such as Christmas carols, even if they are reluctant to join in Christian prayers.

This was the most restrained of the three liturgies that we wrote. Restraint was occasioned partly by the civic and multicultural nature of the service, but also because we wanted to avoid occluding the exuberant dramatic performances that lay at the heart of the service. In the event, these performances enacted the themes of the reinterment events with great power and force, and constituted a magnificent conclusion to a week that had begun with the solemnity of Compline and ended with a joyful dance of celebration and *Magnificat*.

4

Symbol and Choreography of the Reinterment Liturgies for Richard III

Constructing meaningful liturgy means a lot more than finding the right words. It involves many things, among which the following seem to be particularly pertinent for this occasion: giving space to God, connecting with the church's tradition and history, connecting with scripture, with the occasion, time and season and trying to read the need and place of those participating and enabling them to find something inspiring, spiritual, invigorating or enabling introspection, connection and comfort. As always the spoken word is important, but what is sung, proclaimed, dramatized or symbolized is more important. Huge effort went into constructing these liturgies firmly rooted in history and tradition, but nevertheless contemporary, modern and fitting for Leicester at this moment in time. It is noteworthy that the week as a whole has its own narrative as well as every individual act of worship.

Background
It came as a huge surprise how many people felt strongly about the reinterment of Richard III, how many letters the cathedral and diocesan staff, university and city staff as well as ecumenical partners received, many of which making rather passionate statements about people's views. Hence some of the symbolism used in the reinterment celebrations is shaped in response to public pressure rather than by isolated liturgical thinking – these rites and ceremonies clearly fulfilled a public need and

a tension arose between those needs and the inherited way of doing this as church. Although the cathedral in the person of the Dean chaired the group making the final decisions about the reinterment events it became obvious that the University of Leicester, the City and County of Leicester, the Richard III Society and the general public had somewhat different interests and priorities about what should happen. Theologically this was very simple: the cathedral re-interred the human remains of somebody who died and was buried with a proper funeral many years ago. There was no surviving immediate family and no direct mourners. It became apparent very early on that this was not the only narrative, but that in the present culture the Christian understandings of death and life after death are disappearing very quickly and that there is widespread public misunderstanding about what Christians believe.

A prime example of this is the design of the tomb. Originally the Cathedral Chapter was very clear that a ledger stone was the preferred way to mark the grave, being aware that all graves of British monarchs since Georgian times have been marked in this way and that the present Queen's grave will be marked in exactly this way. However, a petition to create a three-dimensional tomb rather than a flat ledger stone received thousands of signatures – enhanced by many letters and emails voicing particular distaste at the idea that people might step on a gravestone and walk over it. This happened at the same time as those of us involved in the building works both in Cathedral Gardens and inside the cathedral building became keenly aware that there are dozens of graves under the present floor of the cathedral, few of them marked.

More has been written about the successful design for the tomb, its placement in a space, which is deliberately not a chapel with an altar, but clearly a space of significance and honour within Leicester Cathedral.

Similar to the tomb design, but less significant, was the use of three different soils: from Bosworth battlefield, from Fotheringhay Castle and from Middleham in Yorkshire, where Richard met his future wife Anne. These were placed within the grave. This happened in response to public

The Language of Liturgy in two ages

imagination and pressure and has no particular liturgical relevance. Arguably, the use of soil from his previous grave, into which most of his body apart from his bones dissolved over 500 years, would have been more significant.

An argument that the Liturgy Group lost was about how Richard's human remains should be buried and in which way the remains of his body should be visibly contained. We argued – in line with archaeological advice and historical and contemporary practice – that the bones should be placed in an ossuary. This would have made a very public and obvious statement that these events were not a funeral of a human body, but a reinterment of human remains. During the building works in Cathedral Gardens I presided over two reinterment services of human remains exhumed during the building works: these were very simple and short, but dignified occasions placing human bones back into sacred ground – deliberately not funeral services but liturgically occasions similar to a Burial of Ashes following a funeral. I was astonished by the passionate display of distaste towards the idea of burying the bones in an ossuary – particularly people arguing that this was disrespectful, unchristian and un-Catholic; despite the burial of the bones of many saints and popes in this way. In response to public feeling the lead ossuary was placed in a wooden coffin, giving the outward impression of a human form.

I continue to be intrigued by the underlying perceptions of human dignity and personhood displayed through public feelings: there was a strong desire to sanitize the stark reality of death and decay and the fact that the feet are missing, and in contrast to Christian theological anthropology a strong desire to humanize the mortal remains and treat them as 'sacred' items.[31]

Everybody involved in these events found themselves embedded within passionate controversy, often in the form of strongly-worded

---

[31] David Monteith: 'Richard III: theological issues' (Lecture to Leicester Theological Society, 16 September 2015).

letters and emails, of personal encounters and of being surprised by the sensitivity of any statement or wording. It was – in hindsight – helpful that the Judicial Review about Richard's final resting place gave those involved in the planning of the liturgical occasions time to think these through properly. Finding oneself within an unexpected storm of controversy made it obvious that 500 years after the Battle of Bosworth, and centuries after the Reformation, the Christian theme of reconciliation needed to be at the core of everything we did around Richard's reinterment. It seemed providential that finding common ground, reconciliation and building community as the Cathedral of the most diverse city in England was at the core of our calling. What we did was influenced by our location and specific calling: I am sure other cathedrals would have done this differently.

Ecumenical Collaboration
Right from the beginning of the archaeological survey the cathedral, the diocese of Leicester, the Roman Catholic diocese of Nottingham, the Archbishop of Canterbury and the Cardinal Archbishop of Westminster received many letters expressing concern. It was most helpful that this resulted in immediate consultation and collaboration, in joint public statements and in sharing some of the more significant or amusing letters (sometimes amusing in hindsight).

From a Roman Catholic perspective Richard III was a Catholic monarch, as he lived and reigned in pre-reformation times. From a Church of England perspective his church was an antecedent of the present Church of England – as it sees itself in unbroken continuity with the Church of this realm before the Reformation back to Augustine of Canterbury. However, it is obvious that the *Ecclesia Anglicana* of the time of Richard was in communion with the See of Rome, whereas the present Church of England currently is not. Although there is a different ecclesiological view of the Church at the time of Richard III, depending on which ecclesiastical tradition one belongs to, there was no theological disagreement about his reinterment and what should happen or what was understood theologically. As his funeral had happened in 1485, predating the Reformation, and he was to be reinterred in consecrated ground, Anglicans and Roman Catholics involved agreed from the very beginning to collaborate as closely and co-operatively as possible in this – recognizing that the life of Richard III preceded the split of communion. All involved were keen to pursue the theme of reconciliation and to make a visible and tangible point in collaborating as closely as possible.

It is noteworthy that this intention survived intense public pressure and media pressure – particularly the latter trying to find discord and newsworthy publishable conflict where there was none.

This extensive collaborative planning was made visible in the preaching of the Cardinal Archbishop of Westminster at the Service of Reception (Compline) on the Sunday in Reinterment Week, through the liturgical presence of the Bishop of Leicester and the Dean of Leicester at the (Roman Catholic) Requiem Mass at Holy Cross Priory on the Monday, through the shared Evening Prayer with the Roman Catholic Dominican Community of Holy Cross Priory and the wider English Dominican Province at Leicester Cathedral on the Tuesday, through the preaching of the Prior of Holy Cross at the Eucharist for the Feast of the Annunciation on the Wednesday presided over by one of the Anglican Franciscan Sisters in Leicester (CSF) and by the presence of the Diocesan Administrator of the diocese of Nottingham (in the absence of a bishop during a vacancy) at the side of the Archbishop of Canterbury at the Reinterment Service. The Roman Catholic and Anglican collaboration exceeded other ecumenical and inter-faith involvement in recognition of the pre-reformation life of King Richard. The relationships built and developed have far surpassed and long survived the reinterment week.

Procession and Reception
The human remains of Richard III showed many wounds – both battle wounds and post mortem mutilations. The controversial idea to repeat

the procession from Bosworth Battlefield to Leicester happened in recognition that something was amiss in 1485: in contrast to the shaming and mutilation of the body of the defeated King the human remains repeated this journey in a way more conscious of the dignity of human bodies, more in keeping with the honour Christians consider appertains to human beings and human remains, and with the particular role of the deceased in history. This was not to rewrite or undo history, but to acknowledge that there was a lack of dignity and honour that hindered reconciliation up to present times. This became strongly apparent when it was announced that descendants of both Yorkist and Lancastrian peers who participated in the Battle of Bosworth were going to be among those who accompanied the coffin as it entered Leicester Cathedral. This was particularly highlighted in the person of the Earl of Derby, a descendant of Lord Thomas Stanley. Stanley's change of allegiance and betrayal of his friend Richard was probably decisive for the outcome of the Battle of Bosworth. Again the controversy around him walking together with other peers, including the current Duke of Gloucester, demonstrated the need for reconciliation and the potential for symbolic gestures and words enabling and supporting this.

The procession from Bosworth to Leicester Cathedral stopped at a number of stations, on some occasions short services accompanied these stops. These took the form of the Daily Office: the medieval rite stressed that the normal services of the church continued during the days of reinterment. Hence the traditional hallowing of time through regular prayer during the day was slightly adapted to make reference to the dead in general and to Richard in particular, though we took great care not to give the impression of repeating funeral liturgies over and over.

With the arrival of the coffin at Leicester Cathedral the tone changed from something fairly cheerful, celebratory and exciting, to something rather sombre. It was impressive to note that a large crowd of people who had gathered to see the arrival of the remains were keeping silence. A simple wooden coffin was received by Bishop and Dean in Cathedral

The Language of Liturgy in two ages

Gardens before the crowd, marking the handing over of responsibility from the University of Leicester to Leicester Cathedral.

Another royal funeral liturgy that is unlikely to be repeated in the foreseeable future is the burial rite of the Royal Family of Austria, enacted for Otto von Habsburg, last Crown-Prince of Austria, who died in 2011. The so-called *Anklopfritual* consists of the Master of Ceremonies knocking on the door of Vienna Cathedral. Questioned by one of the priests who was demanding entry the MC first recites the ancestry and family history of the deceased, stressing the role of the deceased in history. Following this the cathedral clergy reply, 'We do not know him.' Secondly, the MC recites all the titles and honours the deceased received during his or her time of life, and again the clergy reply in the same way. Finally the MC answers the question of who demands entry with a very simple line: 'Otto - a mortal and sinful human being.'[32] Following this line, the clergy open the gates and invite the entry of the procession.

The reception of the mortal remains of King Richard stressed a similar point: he was received as a baptized human being. What matters is not titles and honours, but the dignity of every single human being a citizen of heaven under the equalizing power of death. This was the rationale behind not speaking of 'King' Richard, but using solely his Christian name: 'We receive the remains of our brother Richard with confidence in God, the giver of life, who raised the Lord Jesus from the dead.' The piece of music by John Sheppard (c.1515-1560) accompanying the walk from the cathedral doors to the font affirmed the same theological point:

Media vita in morte sumus:
quem quaerimus adjutorem
nisi te Domine
qui pro peccatis nostris juste irasceris?

---

[32] For wording in German see http://wiev1.orf.at/stories/526472, accessed 08. January 2016.

(In the midst of life we are in death: of whom may we seek for succour but of thee, O Lord, who for our sins art justly displeased?).

The coffin was moved to the font as the place of Christian baptism, stressing the point that a baptized Christian, a citizen of heaven, was being received by the church. This narrative was affirmed through a number of symbolic actions: the processional cross was placed near the coffin, and as a reminder of baptism water was sprinkled on the coffin, with incense used as a sign of prayer. A pall as a sign of the covering love of God was added by the descendants of Bosworth peers, and a fifteenth-century Vulgate bible in the possession of the University of Leicester was placed on top of the coffin. Somewhat controversially, and outside this narrative, a replica of his crown was placed on top of the coffin, deliberately done by a small child from Bosworth – accompanied by a prayer praising Jesus Christ as Lord and King. Tangibly and deliberately, different groups of people contributed during these rites: Bishop and Dean, the Cardinal Archbishop of Westminster, descendants of Bosworth peers, the University Chaplain, members of the cathedral community and a child from the place where he died.

Following this the cathedral community sang the service of Compline as could have happened any day – welcoming the remains of our brother Richard into Leicester Cathedral and doing what the church does: hallowing time by praying the daily office and praying for the church, living and departed.

Repose

On every normal weekday Leicester Cathedral celebrates Morning Prayer, Evening Prayer and the Eucharist. Following the precedent of the medieval rite we continued with these normal services. Offering worship is the prime *raison d'être* of any church. Originally we planned to empty and close the church before any acts of worship and to stop the flow of people past the tomb. However, the number of those wishing to pay their respects was beyond any expectation: between Monday morning and

The Language of Liturgy in two ages

Wednesday lunchtime we welcomed approximately 20,000 people who desired to be part of these events. Hence we continued to allow people to walk past the coffin during acts of worship, but made clear that those coming for worship could not jump the queue by doing so.

Following a similar rationale at the processional station liturgies we did not dramatically change our pattern of worship or its content: we prayed the daily office with particular mention of those visiting and the church living and departed. Similarly the eucharists did not undergo major adjustments: we were in the liturgical time of Passiontide, thus the liturgical season already provided a focus on penitence and death and life after death. Technically the prayers for the departed classified these eucharists as Requiem Eucharists but, in line with the theme of reconciliation, we took care to pray for all those departed at the Battle of Bosworth and for the whole church, living and departed.

The Roman Catholic Requiem Mass with Anglican participation presided over by the Cardinal Archbishop of Westminster took place at Holy Cross Priory, but was published and intended as an integral part of the Reinterment Week. Similarly other churches around city and county used liturgical material that the cathedral published beforehand in their own services – often singing Compline with its overt references to death and dying which lent itself very easily to these occasions.

Reinterment
The actual service of reinterment needed to acknowledge several groups of people and their connection with the archaeological project, Richard III and the Battle of Bosworth. As there were very few speaking roles this was mostly done via formal procession and recession. It obviously included representatives from University, City, those genetically descended from Richard's sister who donated DNA and, deliberately walking together, descendants from peers and commoners who fought at Bosworth.

To recognize the fact that Richard III was the last British monarch who died in battle, the bearer party comprised of members of the Armed Forces. Historically, the military has not played a major role at royal funerals in Britain, and this event was neither a funeral nor a state occasion. The one historic exception was the funeral of Oliver Cromwell. A contemporary account says that the streets, from Somerset House to Westminster Abbey, were guarded by soldiers, placed without a railing, and clad in new red coats, with black buttons, with their ensigns wrapped in cypress. These made a lane, to keep off spectators from crowding the procession. Whilst not a king, at his funeral Cromwell was styled 'His Highness the most Serene and most Illustrious Oliver Cromwell, late Lord Protector of the Commonwealth of England, Scotland, and Ireland, and the Dominions and Territories thereunto belonging' and the budget was said to be £60,000. At a certain point 'his purple velvet was changed for a crown', and in the funeral procession his wax effigy wore a crown.[33]

It is part of the constitutional role of the Archbishop of Canterbury to preside at royal funerals, hence his presence was appropriate (though not necessary) on this occasion. It is noteworthy that ecumenical and interfaith representatives were given processional recognition and seats of honour, but that in the final procession the Roman Catholic representatives, comprising the Diocesan Administrator for Nottingham and the Prior of Holy Cross, were treated as 'home team' – showing the close collaboration of both communions over these events.

It came as a surprise that the medieval rite put the reinterment of human remains not in the context of a Mass but in the framework of Morning Prayer. It assumed that a Requiem Mass had been read, but the actual act of reburying was set within the context of praising God at the beginning of the day. Secondly, there were not many overt references to resurrection and life after death, but the tone remained liminal,

---

[33] http://www.british-history.ac.uk/burton-diaries/vol2/pp516-530 (accessed 17 March 2016).

The Language of Liturgy in two ages

culminating in the Benedictus and its antiphon from John 11 which is still said at funerals, but usually at the beginning:

Jesus said, 'I am the resurrection and the life. Those who believe in me, even though they die, yet they will live, and everyone who lives and believes in me will never die.'

Here it was placed right at the end, after the reinterment. Following long discussions we kept this structure, seeing the events of the entire week as a unity and adding a more outspoken celebration at the end of the week. This also included keeping the Bishop's sermon in the place where the medieval liturgy envisaged a homily: before the reinterment, at a liminal place of insecurity and transition.

At the beginning of the service the bearer party moved the coffin away from the font into the middle of the nave, in the midst of the people, highly visible to the congregation. There the Duke of Gloucester temporarily rejoined Richard III with his own prayer book – recognizing the importance of personal faith in Richard's life. Making the naked and uncovered coffin so highly visible was a powerful *memento mori*, with only a prayer book demonstrating the hope of faith and the fragility of human existence. The Bishop of Leicester preached near the coffin whilst it was in the middle nave. He spoke into this symbol-laden situation from a personal position of vulnerability and insecurity: he had lost his daughter a few weeks before the reinterment. Following the medieval rite the service gave a strong focus on mortality, the limitation and fragility of human life. Newly written music by Judith Bingham accompanied the coffin on its journey to the grave in the ambulatory – only after the reinterment more celebratory tones were audible: Psalm 150, the Benedictus, Carol Ann Duffy's poem and the Dismissal Gospel expressed hope and anticipation of life after death more confidently.

Reveal
Unlike any funeral the rediscovery of the remains of Richard III was not

The Richard III Reinterment Liturgies

about mourning, saying goodbye and loss, but of finding, welcome and celebration. This does not diminish the sense of loss for some who had invested greatly emotionally and in other ways in finding his remains – particularly among members of the Richard III Society there was a profound sense of loss at the reinterment. However, this historic find changed the city and the county, the university and the cathedral in particular. It changed the sense of who they are: a city which is so diverse and often incoherent was greatly affirmed by a tangible sense of history. This sense of change through connecting with history, of horizontal community through vertical connection, influenced the celebration at the end of reinterment week. This also determined that this service was the one with the most local community involvement. It tried to capture a sense of where this community was going, strengthened and encouraged by an encounter with its own past. For this the local Curve theatre was a natural partner.

The way we tried to express this symbolically was through roses. Originally we were somewhat uneasy about using roses, as they were obviously symbolical for the War of the Roses and its fighting parties. However, conversations with different faith and community representatives showed clearly that roses have universally positive connotations: they stand for love, beauty, commitment; they are often gifts between lovers or demonstrate affection; they symbolize purity and holiness. In Christianity there is a strong tradition, starting with Justin Martyr in the second century and elaborated by Sedulius in the fifth century, that makes a connection between roses and the Blessed Virgin Mary. One of her titles in the Loreto Litany is *rosa mystica*, rose without thorns, which identifies her with the rose of Sharon.

The 'Reveal' service used roses in order to demonstrate that times have changed, that this city and this country have moved on since the War of the Roses and that by engaging with the past a new potential for the future can be unlocked. Moving from *Conflict* via *New Beginnings* to *New Life* through a mixture of text, music and dramatic performance the colour of the huge flower display incorporated different colours apart from red and white – showing that different people who have settled here over the centuries added vibrancy and life to this city. The service culminated in the Magnificat – finishing the week with the third great Christian anthem following the Nunc Dimittis on Sunday evening and the *Benedictus* on Thursday morning – imagining life in the Kingdom of God under the rule of Christ, the true King of the universe.

In a city that provides sanctuary for many who have fled war and conflict these images spoke particularly powerfully, and engendered a feeling of accomplishment, pride and hope. This sense of excitement continued with the opening of the cathedral and its finished tomb of King Richard III to a public and the wider city celebration with lights and fireworks in the evening.

Conclusion
In hindsight this narrative pre-empted Easter. Starting in Passiontide with Compline then moving from the liminal to the celebratory worked. But those of us worshipping in Leicester Cathedral needed to turn our eyes towards Holy Week and Easter immediately afterwards. For most of us this meant that we might have been able to turn our eyes, but not our hearts. To repeat the journey from death to life which we had just undertaken with personal and emotional integrity was almost impossible. The Prior of Holy Cross and I had jokingly granted each other dispensation from all Lenten obligations – but it remained a somewhat sad truth that it would have been easier to go on holiday for Holy Week and Easter Week for all who had been involved in the reinterment. Organizing such an event – though connected to the liturgical year but essentially outside it – left the usual pattern of liturgical time and season out of sync.

One of the difficulties of constructing the reinterment was that its symbolism and choreography unfolded over an entire week. However, only a very small group of people were able to attend all main services

The Richard III Reinterment Liturgies

– the 600 tickets for the general public received more than 13,000 applications. How is it possible to construct a narrative over an entire week with which almost nobody can participate in its entirety?

The answer is twofold: Firstly, all services provided a coherent narrative in themselves and were clearly structured to be valid on their own. If they had been stand-alone events, they would have been constructed differently – but they nevertheless felt coherent in themselves.

Secondly, the major symbols and items of all the services were visible to a much wider audience than those attending the Cathedral. Thousands visited the Cathedral in person and millions took part via the media. Within the city it became tangible that communication happens on many different levels that escape explanation or introspection. Being constantly surrounded by extraordinarily excited and even happy people, who, in spite of queuing for up to four hours seemed to enjoy themselves, was infectious. A lot of people voiced surprise at the hugely positive atmosphere during the evening celebration on Friday: In spite of being crowded with thousands of people and a lot of open fires it felt happy, bubbly, confident and extraordinarily safe.

The theme of reconciliation threading through the entire week of events became visible and tangible at the final celebration of Leicester, with the cathedral at the heart of its calling: building the city which is to come.

www.ingramcontent.com/pod-product-compliance
Lightning Source LLC
Chambersburg PA
CBHW021132080526
44587CB00012B/1252